Calligraphy & Stationery Projects

Reader's Digest

The Reader's Digest Association, Inc.
Pleasantville, New York/Montreal/London/Singapore

Contents

Introduction

Inside this book, you will discover a fabulous selection of handmade stationery projects that are simple and quick to make, such as elegant desk accessories, stunning greeting cards, and fun gift wrap. In addition, this book offers straightforward step-by-step instructions to master the art of decorative lettering to enhance any of these creations.

Congratulations

Filled with handy tips and easy alternatives, these projects are based on the ancient art of calligraphy and aim to develop the skills described in the *Techniques* book. Let yourself be guided through more than 20 inspiring projects using eye-catching inks and intricate brushstrokes in gouache and metallic paint.

Marvel at the intense wash behind a framed alphabet picture, and experiment with ways to personalize your own letterhead or party invitation. This book will help you transform a basic keepsake, such as a wedding album or a baby shower card, into a personalized work of art.

A Personal Touch

*Make your home more inviting using
beautifully written numbers on a house plaque,
or create labels for jars and canisters.
Embellish with brushstrokes or stamps to
create designs in your favorite colors.*

Monogram letterhead
in a variety of styles

Handmade stationery has a special quality that displays your creative side. Explore several styles of lettering and layout to achieve your own personal writing paper with matching envelopes.

1. The styles shown right have been created using a selection of nibs for this trial. Experiment with different letter weights to see which you prefer. Write the initials at the top of your letterhead to form a bold statement.

2. This second style shows a vertical border (right) written on textured paper, which gives an attractive broken effect. Using the wide, flat paintbrush, apply a watery blue wash to watercolor paper and leave it to dry. Then mix the gouache into a stronger color and write the initials over the top. Add pen-made diamonds as dividers.

3. The third style (right) uses lighter-weight capitals written with a No. 3.5 nib. Add a flourish—made with one rapid pen stroke—extending from the last letter (see Tip above right).

Tip Flourishes can be somewhat daunting. Practice first using a pencil until you become comfortable and familiar with the design. Flourishes should extend naturally away from the letter and not intrude too closely on the body of the word. When writing the flourish, do not worry about the odd flick of color, if working on an informal piece, on the paper. This will add a lively and vibrant feel to your finished work.

4. This rough idea (below) is written with a fiber-tipped pen to create contemporary hand-drawn initials.

4 \. Write the initials using a No. 3.5 nib, centered on your letterhead. Color the diamonds using gouache in your pen.

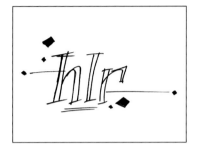

5. For this last style, choose a No. 2.5 nib to write the initials in lowercase italic. Then extend a flourish from the central initial.

5 \. To create the flourish after having written the "l", follow the diagram (below) using the four strokes. Make sure it is no larger than 8 in. (20 cm) so that the design can fit on the back of an envelope.

NOTECARDS AND ENVELOPES
Add your initials to a set of plain cream or white notepaper. Repeat the lettering as a seal on the flap of an envelope.

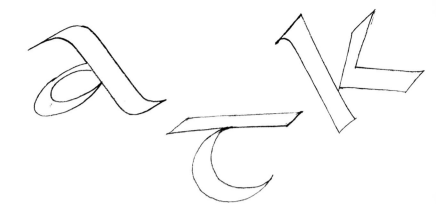

Embossed bookmark
with vertical initials

Embossed lettering creates a soft, subtle design with an elegant feel. This bookmark is made from card stock and is the perfect gift to accompany a best-selling novel.

you will need

- 2 HB lead pencils
- Layout paper
- Scissors and craft knife
- Tracing paper
- Cellophane tape and double-sided tape
- Thin card
- Embossing tool from the set
- Textured watercolor paper, 3 in. x 6 in. (7.5 cm x 15 cm)
- Lilac card, 2½ in. x 7 in. (6 cm x 18 cm)
- Lilac velvet ribbon, 8 in. (20 cm)
- Craft glue

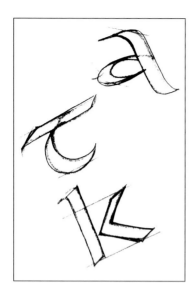

2. Using a sharp pencil and tracing paper, draw around the letters carefully to create the vertical design.

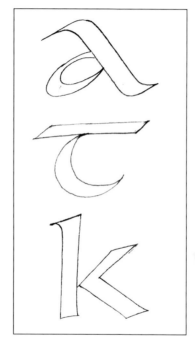

3. Transfer the calligraphy onto a piece of thin card or stencil card. Cut out the letters neatly with a craft knife to form a stencil.

1. Draw your initials on layout paper using two pencils strapped together with an elastic band (see page 21 of the *Techniques* book). Choose a plain alphabet, such as uncial. Cut the letters out individually and move them around until you achieve the correct spacing. Secure them with cellophane tape.

Tip If you have any letters in your initials, such as O, where the center is cut out, either fix the inside edges in place with a small piece of cellophane tape or design a bridge into the letterform (see Tip box on page 34 of the *Techniques* book).

4. Place the stencil facedown on a table and lay a sheet of watercolor paper on top. Using the embossing tool in the set, press the paper around the letter shapes. Remove the paper and trim to form a 2 in. x 5 in. (5 cm x 12.5 cm) rectangle.

5. Glue the paper onto a sheet of lilac card. Trim the card, leaving an ⅛ in. (3 mm) border on three sides. Cut a point at the top.

6. Cut a slit in the pointed end of the card and thread a ribbon through. Secure the ribbon to the back of the card with double-sided tape. Cut a V shape in the end of the ribbon for decoration.

METALLIC FOIL BOOKPLATE
Personalize your diary by using the stencil to emboss your initials onto foil. Mark decorative patterns within the letters using the tip of a ballpoint.

Cookie jar labels
with painted motifs

Make your own label and decorate it with a simple illustration. When baking a batch of cookies, create one label and then scan it into a computer, or use a color photocopier to print extras.

CHERRY COOKIES

From Alice

1. Practice the title in roman capitals using a No. 3.5 nib. Choose a No. 2.5 nib and try foundation lowercase for the ingredients list. Using a variety of colored gouache in your pen, experiment with colors against the paper.

2. To make the fruit illustration, paint a simple shape with the tip of a paintbrush, leaving a white streak as a highlight.

3. Wash the brush and mix a green leaf color. Add the stems and leaves using light brushstrokes. While the red paint is still wet, add a shadow by streaking a thin line of green along the edge opposite the highlight.

Oats, Golden Syrup, Butter, cherries

18

4. Draw faint rules in the appropriate widths to align the title and text. Write the title in the same red paint as the cherries, using your practice sheet as a guide.

5. Switch to the smaller nib and write the remaining text in foundation lowercase with initial capitals. Make sure the two lines are the same length.

Oats, Golden Syrup, butter, cherries. Enjoy!

6. Complete the label by drawing a rule around the edge in green. Run a narrow dip pen along the edge of a ruler. Make sure that the ruler is upside down to prevent the paint from running underneath.

LEMON COOKIE JAR LABEL
Adapt the design to suit different ingredients. Here, green gouache is used for the lettering because the yellow will not show up well against the white paper.

House plaque
with painted numerals

Paint a floral sign for your house using these simple steps. The size of the plaque will partly depend on the length of your number. Drill the wood with countersunk holes before painting the design.

you will need

- Piece of pine, 3½ in. (9 cm) square
- Wood primer
- Sandpaper
- Decorator's paintbrush
- Matte exterior paint (white)
- Two pencils strapped together
- Tracing paper
- Colored chalk pastel
- Masking tape
- No. 2 nylon paintbrush
- Acrylic paints (cadmium yellow, magenta, and ultramarine)

1 2 3 4 5 6 7 8 9 0

2. Using two pencils strapped together, write roman numerals on tracing paper. Thicken up any strokes that are too thin. Position the tracing paper in the center of the wooden plaque and mark its outline on the paper.

1. Paint the wood with primer and a layer of exterior paint. Sand it down between each coat. A matte surface will make it easier to paint the numerals and decoration.

3. On a spare sheet of paper, draw a simple flower or a border of your choice. Transfer the design to the tracing paper, allowing for the screw holes on the plaque.

Tip Think about how you will affix the plaque to a wall. Countersunk screws are used here for simplicity, but if you plan to glue it or use rear fasteners, you will not need to incorporate the holes into your design.

4. Rub a layer of chalk pastel over the back of the tracing paper. Fix the paper to the wood with masking tape and transfer the design using a sharp pencil.

5. Use a No. 2 brush to paint the numbers. If you are an experienced calligrapher, you may prefer to use a broad-edged brush. Repeat to create several layers, allowing each to dry between coats.

6. Paint the border. Here, for example, apply the yellow paint first and leave to dry, then paint in the fine outlines and detail. Add an outline of leaves on either side.

Make a plaque from contrasting colors to match the exterior of your home. This example shows just one of the many borders you could design to add a unique touch to your number plaque.

Desk accessories
wrapped in paper

Brighten up your desk by making your own storage system. A magazine and pen holder are always useful, but you can use this technique to cover all kinds of stationery items.

1. Stretch the cream paper (see note on page 41 in the *Techniques* book). Using a wide, flat brush, paint pale green stripes at regular intervals across the paper. Leave to dry.

2. Using a dragonfly stamp and black ink pad, stamp an irregular pattern all over the paper, overlapping the images onto the green stripes.

3. Cover the thin edges of the magazine holder with a strip of cream paper. To do this, measure the width of the holder and transfer the outline to the center of your strip. Make sure the strip is long enough to cover one side. Cut slits, as shown below, on either side of the lines to allow the paper to bend.

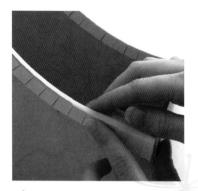

4. Apply double-sided tape to the back of the strip and, starting at one end, press it onto the edge. Fold down the flaps on either side to keep it in place. Trim off excess and repeat with the other, curved side and inside the circular finger hole in front.

Tip For more intricate shapes, it is a good idea to make a white paper template first. This will allow you to test that the shape is correct before spoiling your patterned paper.

5. Lay the patterned paper facedown and place the side of the magazine holder on top. Draw around it carefully to match the curve. Roll the holder onto its long end and draw around it again. Add a 1 in. (2.5 cm) margin to all sides except the curved edge. Cut out with a craft knife.

6. Secure the side panel onto the holder, curved side first, with double-sided tape. Run your fingers along the corners to make sharp creases, but do not stick them down yet. Cut a triangle shape at the base to form two flaps. Press the end panel in place. Fold up the flaps and secure. Trim the top flap, making sure that it covers the edge.

7. Repeat the process for the two remaining sides, cutting off excess paper on the ends and finger hole. Line it with green paper, measuring as before but omitting the top flaps. Cut a rectangle to fit into the base.

STRIPED PEN POT
Make a matching pen holder using the same technique. Cut a strip of patterned paper to match the height and the circumference of the cylinder, and secure it with double-sided tape.

The Hand of Friendship

*Show a friend how much you care with
a personalized gift wrapped in handmade
paper. Greeting cards are especially
appreciated when you have dedicated
the time to making them yourself.*

FRIENDSHIP IS ALWAYS A SWEET RESPONSIBILITY, NEVER AN OPPORTUNITY

Keepsake folder
with friendship motto

Create this stylish folder to give to a friend. Use the paper included in the set, together with the leather cording, calligraphy pen, and ink to complete this project. Use this motto, or add your own message.

- Nib holder and reservoir
- Nos. 0, 2.5, and 3.5 roundhand nibs
- Black ink
- Pencil
- Ruler
- Cream handmade paper, 6¾ in. x 9¾ in. (17 cm x 24.5 cm)
- Green paper, 4 in. x 5½ in. (10 cm x 14 cm)
- Leather cording

1. Using the pen holder and three nibs in the set, practice writing a variety of scripts, giving heavier weight to some words more than others. Use the alphabet sheets to create accurate letters with the correct nib widths.

FRIENDSHIP IS ALWAYS A SWE

2. Draw parallel lines of the same depth on the green paper. The motto is written in uncial, so the spacing between the lines needs to be single because there are minimal ascenders and descenders to consider. Write the focus word using a No. 3.5 nib, then write lightweight lettering for the remaining text.

3. Keep checking that the design is centered on the page with each new line of writing. The use of two weights of lettering produces a visually interesting block of text. For added interest you could try small nib-width patterns at the top and bottom.

FRIENDSHIP IS ALWAYS A SWEET RESPONSIBILITY, NEVER AN OPPORTUNITY

Tip Use a soft putty eraser to remove pencil lines. Hard erasers may rub away the top surface of the paper.

4. Moisten the edges of the paper and tear to create soft edges. Fold the paper at 4 in. (10 cm) and 8½ in. (21.5 cm) away from the left-hand edge. Cut a semicircle ⅝ in. (1.5 cm) in from the top and bottom edge in the center of the largest panel.

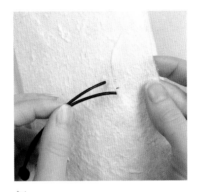

5. Make two holes halfway down the right-hand side of the folder for the leather cord. Tie a knot in the cord and then thread the two loose ends through the folder from the outside. Tie a knot in each end and trim off the excess.

6. Repeat the process to make a loop on the right-hand side, without the knot at the beginning, and tie the two ends together. Insert your written motto by carefully slotting the paper underneath the two semicircular tabs.

A GOOD FRIEND
is hard to find, hard to lose, and impossible to forget.

QUOTATIONS AND MOTTOS
Refer to books or the Internet for alternative poems or quotations.

Greeting cards
for any occasion

These simple brushstroke greeting cards are ideal for an anniversary, birthday, or simply to say thank you. Vary the patterns for each event and tailor the colors to match the recipient.

you will need

- No. 2 sable paintbrush
- Chinese paper
- Gouache (light green and dark green)
- Neutral handmade paper, 4 in. x 6½ in. (10 cm x 16.5 cm)
- Spray adhesive
- Ruler
- Green handmade paper, 4 in. x 6½ in. (10 cm x 16.5 cm)
- Green card, 6½ in. x 8 in. (16.5 cm x 20 cm)
- Pen holder and reservoir
- No. 2.5 roundhand nib
- Green ink

1. To paint the leaves, use the No. 2 sable paintbrush. First, lightly stroke the stem lines across the Chinese paper in the dark green.

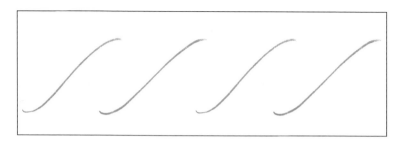

2. Make the fronds by pulling the brush from a light to heavier stroke. Slow down at the same time so that the paint sinks into the absorbent paper. Follow the line of natural growth from the stem.

3. Change color for the other side of the stem. Add a border, top and bottom, in both light and dark green. Leave to dry.

Tip Keep the hairs of your paintbrush parallel with the stroke you are drawing to achieve an even width. You may need to manipulate the brush, your wrist, and the Chinese paper to achieve this.

4. Trim the leaf design to measure 6½ in. (16.5 cm) long, with a thin margin outside the painted border. Mount it onto neutral paper with glue. Using the edge of a ruler, tear the neutral paper, leaving an ⅛ in. (3 mm) border on either side.

5. Glue the neutral paper onto green handmade paper and trim, leaving the same width margin as before. Fold the green card in half to produce a landscape-shaped card. Glue the layered papers onto the middle of the card.

6. Using your alphabet sheets and the wording below as a guide, write a message inside your card with a No. 2.5 nib and green ink.

Thinking of you BEST WISHES

Congratulations

SINGLE FLOWER CARD
Use the same brushstroke technique to create a branching single flower for a square card.

Holiday cards
in seasonal designs

With so many people on your holiday list, it is hard to find a card appropriate for everyone. Instead, tailor your design for friends and family. Here are two cards that will suit many people throughout the season.

you will need

NOEL CARD
- White watercolor paper, 5 in. x 10 in. (12.5 cm x 25 cm)
- H or HB lead pencil
- Tracing paper
- Nos. 00, 0, 2, and 4 paintbrushes
- Gouache (primary red, ultramarine, deep green, white, and gold)
- Ruling pen

SNOWFLAKE CARD
- Linen-weave paper, 5 in. x 10 in. (12.5 cm x 25 cm)
- Stencil card
- Embossing tool
- Cellulose acetate, 3 in. x 6 in. (7.5 cm x 15 cm)
- Double-sided tape
- Snowflake confetti
- White paper, 5 in. x 10 in. (12.5 cm x 25 cm)

NOEL CARD

1. Fold the watercolor paper in half to form a blank card. Section the cover into four equal squares using the ruling pen and gold gouache. Trace the letters at the bottom of this page and transfer the outline of NOEL onto the card as shown.

2. Using the photograph as a guide, fill in the areas that are gold. When dry, place a light wash of red or green over each initial. To create an intense color, apply a second layer of paint while the original layer is still wet. Do not worry if paint goes over the gold, because any ragged lines will be corrected in the final stage of outlining.

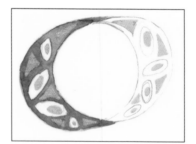

3. Add the colors for the decorative features. Using the finest paintbrush, add white highlights and outline any detailing. Draw an outline around each finished initial.

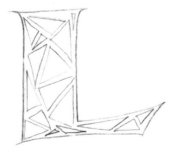

1. Fold the linen-weave paper in half to make a square card. Find the center and cut out a 2¼ in. (5.5 cm) square on the front of the card. Make a stencil to emboss an ⅛ in. (3 mm) border around the aperture (see page 34 in the *Techniques* book), measuring 3 in. x 3 in. (7.5 cm x 7.5 cm).

2. Cut the cellulose acetate into two 3 in. (7.5 cm) squares. Secure one piece behind the aperture inside the card front using double-sided tape. Place the second piece of cellulose acetate behind, securing it down on three edges only. Insert snowflakes between the two layers and seal the remaining edge.

Season's Greetings

3. Line the inside of the card with white paper, cutting out a square aperture to match the window in the front of the card. Finally, write a festive message inside.

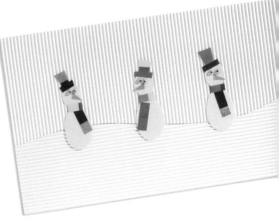

JOLLY SNOWMEN CARD

Make this fun holiday card from textured corrugated paper. Choose printed papers for the hats, scarves, and carrots.

Special Valentines

handmade with love

Valentine's Day is a very personal celebration. Make a unique card for your special someone to let them know just how much you care.

2. Tear a 5 in. x 7 in. (12.5 cm x 18 cm) rectangle of magenta paper. Glue it to the front of the card. Fold over a 1 in. (2.5 cm) margin on the left-hand side of the stamped paper. Attach to the card.

1. Fold the white card into a 5 in. x 7 in. (12.5 cm x 18 cm) rectangle. Use the stamps to print a design on the white paper. Cut the paper to measure 4 in. x 5 in. (10 cm x 12.5 cm).

3. Tear a rough edge along the right-hand side of the tissue paper. Glue in place over the wording.

4. Tear a 2½ in. x 3 in. (6 cm x 7.5 cm) pale pink square and a small 1 in. x 1¼ in. (2.5 cm x 3 cm) heart. Tear a slightly larger magenta heart. Glue the hearts onto the square and secure the brad centrally. Glue the motif to the right-hand side of the card.

Tip To make the curled ends on the small wire heart, wrap a short length of wire around the end of a knitting needle. Then pull it into a spiral.

2. Cut a 9 in. (25 cm) length of wire and shape it into a heart. Thread on the beads and glue in place randomly. Glue the heart in the center of the card.

1. Fold the white watercolor paper in half to make a 3½ in. x 7 in. (9 cm x 20 cm) card. Glue a piece of black handmade paper, 2¼ in. x 8 in. (5.5 cm x 20 cm), to the front of the card on the left-hand side.

3. Punch three hearts from the white handmade paper and glue them evenly in the center of the card. Bend the remaining wire into a small heart (see Tip opposite) and glue in place.

STOLEN-HEARTS CARD
Make a simple heart card by gluing "squares" and dotted ribbon onto a handmade paper card. Stamp three spotted hearts, overlapping the squares.

Gift wrap
decorated with calligraphy

Different-sized nibs produce varying effects on this delightful packaging. The bag displays foundation lettering, but the gift wrap includes several alphabet styles.

you will need

GIFT BAG
- Pink gift wrap, 14 in. x 26 in. (36 cm x 66 cm)
- Ruler and pencil
- Double-sided tape
- 1½ in. (3.5 cm) wide black ribbon, 30 in. (76 cm)
- Layout paper
- Pen holder and reservoir
- Nos. 1.5, 2.5, 3.5 roundhand nibs
- Black ink

CHILD'S GIFT WRAP
- Ivory paper
- Ruler
- H lead pencil
- Penholder and reservoir
- Nos. 1.5 and 3.5 roundhand nibs
- Gouache (primary red, ultramarine, Naples yellow, and zinc white)
- Palette
- No. 5 automatic pen (see page 8 in the *Techniques* book)

1. Using the template below, mark the fold lines on the reverse of the bag. Using a ruler, fold all the dotted lines. Turn the paper over and fold the dashed lines to form the inside folds.

2. Apply double-sided tape along edge A and secure it to edge AA, making sure that the bag is able to fold flat.

3. Fold edge B inside the top. Fold in edge C to make the base of the bag. Add double-sided tape along the 45-degree edge at the bottom of the bag. Press together.

4. Cut two 1 in. (2.5 cm) slots, one above the other, in the center of the bag ¼ in. (6 mm) apart, with the lower slot ¾ in. (2 cm) away from the top edge. Thread the ribbon through and tie a bow.

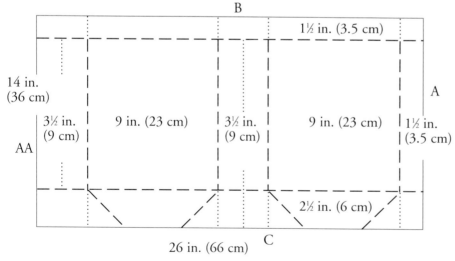

B

1½ in. (3.5 cm)

14 in. (36 cm)

A

3½ in. (9 cm) 9 in. (23 cm) 3½ in. (9 cm) 9 in. (23 cm) 1½ in. (3.5 cm)

AA

2½ in. (6 cm)

26 in. (66 cm) C

5. Draw lines ½ in. (1 cm) apart over the lower half of your bag. Use lowercase lettering throughout to give an even texture. Experiment on layout paper with different-sized nibs to give varying effects.

happy birthday

bonne   bonne

compleanno

compleanno

Tip Carefully work out the order of the phrases and the size of the nibs. Make sure that you always accommodate the ascenders and descenders in the layout to avoid clashing letters.

6. Use a No. 2.5 nib to write "feliz cumpleaños." Separate the phrases with a small pen-made diamond.

feliz cumpleaños ·

7. Use a No. 1.5 nib for "bonne anniversaire."

bonne anniversaire ·

8. Use a No. 3.5 nib for "happy birthday."

happy birthday

9. Repeat the order of nib sizes and write the phrases on the bag. Continue until you have filled all of the lines. Repeat on the opposite side.

feliz cumpleaños · feliz cumpleaños · feliz cu
bonne anniversaire · bonne anniver
happy birthday · happy birthday · happy birthday ·
buon compleanno · buon compleanno · buon
feliz cumpleaños · feliz cumpleaño
bonne anniversaire · bonne anniversaire · bonne anni
happy birthday · happy birthday · happy bi
buon compleanno · buon complea
feliz cumpleaños · feliz cumpleaños · feliz cumpl
bonne anniversaire · bonne anniversaire · bon

1. Using a large sheet of ivory-colored paper, draw sufficient boxes to cover the area. These should measure 3 in. x 3 in. (7.5 cm x 7.5 cm), and have a 1½ in. (3.5 cm) margin around each one. Position the boxes so that they appear to be diamond-shaped.

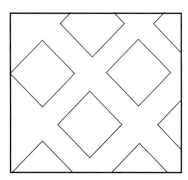

2. Work systematically along each line of writing to avoid smudges. Start with a No. 1.5 nib and write from A to H along the top left-hand side of the first square.

3. Use a No. 3.5 nib for the next box, and alternate in this manner along the first line of boxes. Choose alternate colors for each box and attempt a few color changes as you write.

Tip Use a right triangle for drawing the squares. This will help you draw constant margins between the squares, and make sure the corners are at 90° angles.

4. Use a No. 3.5 nib to write the numbers along the second line of boxes. Again, start at the top left-hand side of each box.

1·2·3·4·5·6·7·8·9·0

5. Once all of the lettering on the left-hand side is complete, turn the sheet of paper and begin writing along the second side of the box. Continue in the same manner as before until all the outside lettering and numbers are complete. Leave to dry.

6. Using an automatic pen, place a single letter of the alphabet or a number in the center of each box.

7. Finally, use a No. 1.5 nib to create decorative lines between the boxes. Follow the length of the box, filling in the space created in the center with a pen-made diamond using the automatic pen.

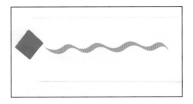

Weddings
and Special Occasions

Family events and personal milestones are occasions worth celebrating. Use your calligraphy skills to make a set of wedding stationery for a friend or to welcome a new arrival.

Reception
Directions
R.S.V.P

Save the Date
For the wedding of
Samantha Willis and Scott Farrell
Saturday, 11th August, 2007
The Drake Hotel, Chicago

Mr and Mrs Paul Edward Willis
request the pleasure of your company
at the marriage of their daughter
Samantha Willis
to
Scott Andrew Farrell

Saturday
11th August, 2007
The Drake Hotel,
Chicago

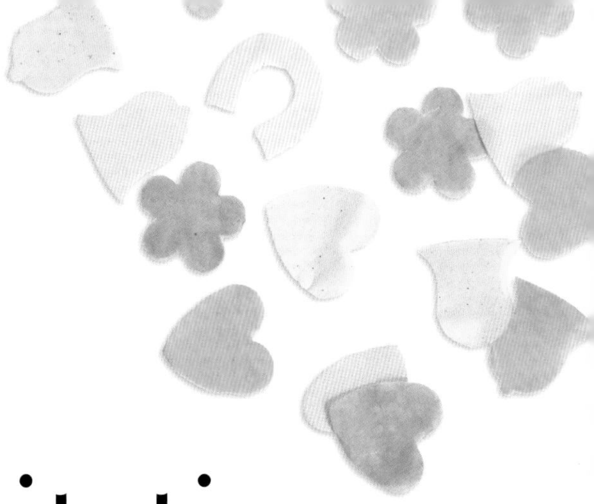

Wedding invitation
embellished with confetti

This special wedding invitation makes a lovely memento, and its case keeps all of the important information together for the big day.

you will need

- Layout paper
- Ruler and pencil
- Copperplate nib and ink
- Watercolor paper
- Orange card, 12 in. x 16 in. (30 cm x 40 cm) and 6½ in. x 7 in. (16.5 cm x 18 cm)
- Paper glue and double-sided tape
- White handmade paper
- White ribbon, 16 in. (40 cm)
- Confetti

1. Write all the information for the invitation on layout paper. Do not worry if you make mistakes, because you will be cutting up the text to paste onto your layout later.

Samantha Willis

Mr an M Mr and Mrs Paul Edward Willis
request the pleasure of your company at the marriage of their daughter
to Saturday, the eleventh day of August, Two thousand and seven
At three o'clock in the afternoon The S Drake St Hotel

2. Write the names of the couple to be married in a larger letter size than the rest of the information. As a guide, the height of the capitals is about ⁵⁄₁₆ in. (8 mm).

Mr and Mrs Paul Edward Willis
request the pleasure of your company

3. Leaving a generous interline space, make a pasteup with the text in a centered design. Set aside.

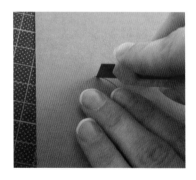

4. Score two folds, 7 in. (18 cm) and 14 in. (36 cm) away from the left-hand side, on the large piece of orange card. Position the paper for the invitation on top of the central panel. Mark the positions of the semicircular tabs that hold the paper. Cut with a craft knife.

Tip To make a large batch of invitations, use a photocopier to transfer the wording onto your paper. By doing this, you then have the option of writing larger letters for the pasteup, which can then be reduced to your required size.

6. Tear a sheet of watercolor paper to a height of 11¾ in. (29 cm). Position it so that the deckle edge is slightly longer than the orange card on the right-hand side. Score, fold, and trim, then wrap it around the orange card.

5. Measure ½ in. (1 cm) away from the bottom and side edges of the remaining orange card. Score along the lines and trim the corners to form flaps. Cut a curved shape at the top of the card and two semicircular tabs. Fold over the flaps and secure to the folder with double-sided tape.

7. Cut a slot in the flap of white paper and thread the ribbon through. Secure with cellophane tape to the back of the overlap. Glue confetti to the outside of the folder. Cut a 6 in. x 9 in. (15 cm x 23 cm) piece of watercolor paper for the invitation. Decorate with confetti. Repeat to make additional invitation items.

8. Using your pasteup as a guide, write the final invitation on the confetti paper. Repeat for the other invitation items.

TYING THE KNOT
Close the invitation by tying the ribbon in a bow.

Place cards
for the perfect meal

Add a personal touch to your reception or dinner party by making a place card for each guest. Then write the name in a color that complements your linen.

you will need

- Pencil
- Putty eraser
- Nib holder and reservoir
- No. 2.5 roundhand nib

RAISED HEART
- White linen-weave card, 3 in. x 3½ in. (7.5 cm x 9 cm)

SILVER LEAVES
- Silver card, 3 in. x 4 in. (7.5 cm x 10 cm)
- Watercolor paper, 2¾ in. x 3¾ in. (7 cm x 9.5 cm)
- 2 skeleton leaves

PINK HEART
- Watercolor paper, 1½ in. x 6 in. (3.5 cm x 15 cm)
- Scrap of pink handmade paper

1. Mark a central line on the linen-weave card as a fold line. Draw a heart, with internal detailing, in the center of the fold line so that the heart hangs downward.

2. Cut around the heart above the fold line only. Then cut out the two detail lines inside the heart to make a filigree design. Score and fold the card along the drawn line without folding the heart. Using a No. 2.5 nib, write the name under the heart shape. Erase pencil lines.

3. Glue the watercolor paper to the center of the silver card. Position the two skeleton leaves to form a heart shape. Trim with scissors if necessary. Glue in place. Write the name under the leaves using a No. 2.5 nib.

KATE EDWARDS

Louise Marks

1. Mark a fold line 1½ in. (3.5 cm) from the left-hand edge of a piece of watercolor paper. Fold over to form a plain card.

ADDING THE NAMES

Using a No. 2.5 nib, practice names on layout paper. Here you can see upper and lowercase italic and uncial. Find the central points and draw a faint line on the place cards, leaving room for ascenders and descenders. Mark the start and end points of the names. Write them in ink and erase the lines.

2. Cut a pink heart no larger than ¾ in. (2 cm) high from heavyweight handmade paper. Glue the heart onto the short end of the folded card.

3. Draw a line on the white card above and below the heart, in line with the center. Cut along this line and around the right-hand side of the card. Add the name to the long side of the card.

James Stanley

Mark Arthur

Wedding album
handmade to cherish

This simple but elegant album makes a special gift or can be a wonderful addition to your own collection. Include a large selection of pages for photos or for keeping a written record to celebrate the day over and over.

you will need

- 2 sheets of white card and 8 sheets each of watercolor paper and tissue paper, 10 in. x 11½ in. (25 cm x 29 cm)
- Hole punch
- 8 sheets of watercolor paper, 2 in. x 10 in. (5 cm x 25 cm)
- Spray adhesive
- Thin white card, 9½ in. x 10 in. (24 cm x 25 cm)
- 2 sheets of white handmade paper
- Heart-shaped punch
- White cord, 1½ yd. (1.5 m)

1. Mark the positions of the holes on two sheets of white card, eight sheets of watercolor paper, and the tissue paper. Space them in two columns of eight, 1 in. (2.5 cm) apart, and then 1½ in. (3.5 cm) away from the top and ½ in. (1 cm) in from the left-hand edge. Punch the holes. Repeat for the thin strips of watercolor paper.

2. Make a hinge for the front cover by scoring through the reverse side of one sheet of white card, 2 in. (5 cm) from the left-hand side. Cut a 3¼ in. (8 cm) square to make the recess in the center of the cover. Glue the thin card to the inside of the cover to conceal the aperture.

3. Wrap both covers in handmade paper, making sure that the paper fits into the recess on the front cover. Cut through the paper over the holes. Glue the excess to hide the edge of the card.

5. Starting at the fifth hole down on the right, thread the white cord from back to front and then through each hole, making a crisscross pattern on the front of the album. Tie the ends together in a knot at the back and trim the excess.

4. Using the heart punch, punch a heart in the bottom right-hand corner on each page. Starting with the back cover, assemble the album with tissue paper and a thin paper strip between each page.

6. Make a quantity of pink paper pulp into a heart motif (see page 44 in the *Techniques* book). When dry, glue to the recess on the front cover.

Birthday celebrations
cards and invitations

Use bright papers and coordinated paints to create lively birthday cards and party invitations. These examples use simple letters in a number of fun ways. Choose colors and alphabets to suit your event.

you will need

21ST BIRTHDAY CARD
- Thick paper or card in red, orange, and yellow
- Glue stick
- Nib holder and reservoir
- No. 1.5 roundhand nib
- Gouache (scarlet and alizarin)
- Palette
- Imitation gold paint
- Ruler, pencil, and eraser

50TH BIRTHDAY CARD AND PARTY INVITATION
- Gouache (magenta and scarlet)
- Nib holder and reservoir
- Nos. 1.5 and 2.5 roundhand nibs
- Card in red, orange, yellow, and purple
- Glue stick
- Paintbrush

2. Arrange the squares so that they overlap in a trio of diamond shapes. Glue in place. For additional decoration, add gold lines to emphasize the central square. Outline the edges in gold.

1. Draw lines at right angles on two squares of yellow paper and one square of orange paper. Using a No. 1.5 nib, write roman numerals on the orange square four times, turning the paper each time. Use alternating colors and always start from the central point. Write the numerals three times on each yellow square. Cut three more squares, ¼ in. (6 mm) wider than the first, to form borders.

3. Make random diamond patterns across the front of the card in gold. Use large and small pen-made nib width squares to create a bubble effect like champagne.

What went wrong? If your colored numerals do not show up against the colored paper, you may have mixed in too much water; add more gouache from the tube and mix it to a thicker consistency, possibly adding a tiny amount of white to give the red color more body.

PARTY INVITATION

1. Lightly mark three curved pencil lines on the front of the card. Using the lines as guides, write "PARTY." Use a No. 1.5 nib and uppercase foundation letters. Repeat with a No. 2.5 nib in a lighter color.

2. Lightly mark the positions of the words "We're having a" in pencil before writing the straight lettering. When the gouache is dry, use a fine brush to add the swirly paper streamers. Use several colors and position them across the front of the card.

50TH BIRTHDAY CARD

1. Write "50" as large as possible in one color. Then write a shadow repeat. This will make the number stand out by enlarging its presence.

2. Draw a flame shape on three pieces of card. Make the orange shape the largest, and then decrease the size for the red and purple. Assemble the flame and glue together. Using the photograph as a guide, arrange the candle on the front of your card.

to announce
the arrival of

Sophie

on 28th May
weighing 7 lb 6 oz

Baby occasions
with precious details

Having a baby is a momentous occasion that deserves the warmest welcome. This framed calligraphy panel is a fabulous way to celebrate a new arrival.

BABY ANNOUNCEMENT

- Nib holder and reservoir
- Nos. 1.5 and 3.5 roundhand nibs
- White card, 8½ in. x 11 in. (21.5 cm x 28 cm)
- Gouache (alizarin rose madder mixed with zinc white)
- Pink parchment paper
- White mountboard
- Baby's hands stamp

BABY SHOWER CARD

- Square metallic lilac paper, 2¾ in. (7 cm)
- Square lilac gingham paper, 3 in. (7.5 cm) plus scrap
- Circle of lilac paper, 2 in. (5 cm) diameter
- Square white card, 4½ in. (11.5 cm)
- 2 lilac buttons
- Flower embellishment

to announce the arrival of

1. Draw rules ¼ in. (5 mm) in height. Using a No. 3.5 nib, write the information in italic upper and lowercase on a sheet of layout paper.

SOPHIE

Sophie

s·o·p·h·i·e

2. Use a No. 1.5 nib to write the child's name. To create an informal-looking name, do not draw center rules, and leave room for a couple of flourishes. As a guide, the size of the body of this lettering, above, is ⅝ in. (1.5 cm) high.

to announce the arrival of

Sophie

3. Make a pasteup once you have written all of the text. Leave an interline space of ½ in. (1.5 cm) between the lowercase text, and an empty space of approximately 1½ in. (4 cm) above the next writing line. Include a similar space to the writing underneath the name. This placement of the child's name is flexible because of the variations of letters in every name.

Tip To eradicate the general fear of making an error when writing a final piece of calligraphy, it is a good idea to draw rules on several pieces of parchment. Then if you make a mistake, you can easily move onto the next sheet. Practice until you are happy with the look of the name and its relationship to the lowercase italic lettering. Experiment with other styles of alphabet if you prefer.

4. Transfer your design onto parchment. Draw up the rules, marking each line length. Write the text in the order that it appears, to avoid having to wait for the lettering to dry. Cut the mountboard to size; then cut an aperture in the center, slightly larger than your lettering. Use a stamp in the shape of two baby's hands to add an embellishment.

1. Glue the metallic lilac paper centrally onto the gingham square. Using the photograph as a guide, cut out a quadrant from the lilac circle. Glue the shape onto the metallic paper. Add the trim.

2. Glue the design centrally onto the watercolor card. Using strong adhesive or glue dots, secure the flower and the two buttons for the carriage wheels.

IT'S A BOY!
Blue parchment and blue gouache are the way to go when making this gift.

Tip Wait until the paint is completely dry before you erase the ruled pencil lines. Work very cautiously because some color pigments smudge more easily than others.

Cherished Keepsakes

Freestyle letters break all the rules and,
along with stylish materials, enable
stationers to create unique projects.
Make cherished photograph albums, or
try your hand at marbling paper.

Marbled papers
and simple bookplate

Marbled papers are fun to make because the result is unique every time. These endpapers are enhanced by a simple bookplate that offers your project a classic feel.

you will need

- Nib holder and reservoir
- Nos. 2.5 and 3.5 roundhand nibs
- Layout paper
- Repositionable glue
- Gouache (alizarin crimson, olive green, and yellow ochre)
- Paintbrush
- Palette
- Marbling bath and inks
- White paper
- Spray adhesive

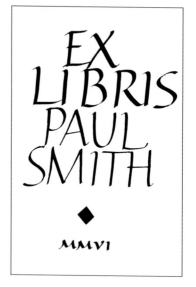

1. Create sheets of marbled paper (see page 40 of the *Techniques* book) larger than one spread (two pages) of the book you want to line.

EX LIBRIS   EX·LIBRIS
ex libris   Ex Libris
PAUL PAUL   mmvi
mmvi EX LIBRIS   PAUL SM
SMITH

2. Practice various styles of lettering for the wording on the bookplate. Here, the uppercase foundation alphabet is used throughout.

3. Use a No. 2.5 nib for the words "Ex Libris," and a No. 3.5 for the name and date.

EX
LIBRIS
PAUL
SMITH
◆
MMVI

Tip When choosing an appropriate paint color for the letters on the bookplate, use a shade that will complement or match the tones in the marbled paper.

5. Transfer the measurements to the final paper and write the text. Use a contrasting color when adding the decorative diamond, and another color for the border lines. Trim to size.

4. The overall size of this bookplate is 3 in. x 4½ in. (7.5 cm x 11.5 cm). All rules are drawn at a measurement of ⅛ in. (3 mm), with a 1/16 in. (2 mm) interline space. Make a pasteup of your layout in order to accurately gauge the length of the writing lines.

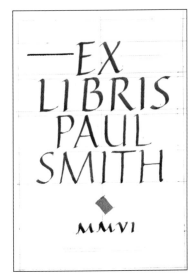

6. Measure the existing endpapers in your book. Cut the marbled paper accurately to match. Glue the marbled paper over the endpapers with spray adhesive. Position the bookplate in the center of the right-hand page and glue into position.

MARBLED GIFT BOXES
Make a set of mini gift boxes by covering small store-bought papier mâché boxes with marbled papers.

Photo frame
embellished with beads

*Delicate handmade paper
decorated with dried flower
petals is teamed up with
gleaming rocaille beads for
a charming photo frame.*

you will need

- White card, 8½ in. x 11 in. (21.5 cm x 28 cm)
- 2 sheets of cream handmade paper, 8½ in. x 11 in. (21.5 cm x 28 cm)
- Double-sided tape
- Needle
- Cream thread
- Cellophane tape
- Gold rocaille beads
- Cream card

1. On a piece of white card, mark out the basic frame shape by measuring an outer square of 5 in. x 6 in. (12.5 cm x 15 cm) and an inner square of 3 in. x 4 in. (7.5 cm x 10 cm). Draw a scalloped edge around the outside of the frame. Cut out with a craft knife. Secure to the back of the handmade paper with double-sided tape.

2. Cut a 2 in. x 3 in. (5 cm x 7.5 cm) aperture from the cream handmade paper. Make a 45-degree cut at each of the corners to form tabs. Fold the tabs through the aperture and onto the back of the frame. Secure with double-sided tape and trim around the scalloped edge.

3. Thread a needle with the cream thread. Secure the end in one corner on the back of the card with cellophane tape. Thread on the beads until the string is long enough to fill one side of the aperture. Secure the string of beads in the adjacent corner to keep it tight along the edge. Repeat to complete the remaining three sides of the aperture.

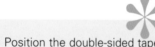

Tip Position the double-sided tape on the cream mount so it encroaches onto the frame area slightly. Then use this to secure the beads more firmly in place.

4. Cut a cream mount, 4 in. x 5 in. (10 cm x 12.5 cm), with an inside aperture of 2 in. x 3 in. (5 cm x 7.5 cm). Stick this in place centrally to the back of the frame. Make sure that the beads are clearly seen on the front. Glue the other piece of cream handmade paper to the back of the frame. Trim around the inner and outer edges.

5. Make the back by cutting another piece of card 4½ in. x 5¾ in. (11.5 cm x 14.5 cm) with a V section at the top. Cover the back of this with cream paper, as on the frame. Secure along the base and two sides with double-sided tape.

6. Finish with a paper-covered stand made from a 1½ in. x 4 in. (3.5 cm x 10 cm) piece of card. Slant the bottom edge to enable the frame to stand.

PICTURE PERFECT
Use this technique to create any shaped frame, from a simple square to a more elaborate heart shape. Vary the colored paper and beads to suit your room scheme.

Photo album
with embossed panel

Keep your photographs safe in this classic album. The handmade paper cover has a textured appearance, and the black pages display digital or traditional prints to their best advantage.

you will need

- 2 sheets of foam board, 6½ in. x 10 in. (16.5 cm x 25 cm), for covers
- Black card for pages, 6½ in. x 10 in. (16.5 cm x 25 cm)
- Waxed paper for interleaves, 6½ in. x 10 in. (16.5 cm x 25 cm)
- Black card strips, two for each page, 1½ in. x 6½ in. (3.5 cm x 16.5 cm)
- Double-sided tape
- 4 sheets of terra-cotta handmade paper, 8½ in. x 11 in. (21.5 cm x 28 cm)
- Natural raffia, 24 in. (60 cm)

2. Glue the black card strips along the left-hand edge, one below and one above, on the sheets of waxed paper to make interleaves. Punch holes to correspond with the pages. Stack the pages alternately with the interleaves. Set aside.

1. Decide how many pages you want in your album and then count out the number of black pages, waxed paper, and black card strips according to the materials list on page 85. Measure 1½ in. (3.5 cm) in from the left-hand side of the black card pages and score along the line. This will enable the pages to fold. Position a hole punch centrally within this area and punch holes.

3. Using one piece of foam board, measure 1½ in. (3.5 cm) from the left-hand side. Score through the top layer to make a hinge. Turn the foam board over to form the front cover.

Tip When scoring the hinge on the front cover, make a light cut with a craft knife without putting much pressure on the foam board. You want to cut only through the top layer.

4. Mark the holes on the covers and cut with a craft knife. Cover both sides of the back cover with handmade paper. Cut the paper where it overlaps the holes and push it down to cover the white edges.

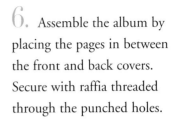

5. Repeat the process for the front cover. Trim the handmade paper to measure 10 in. (26 cm) wide to avoid excess paper getting stuck in the hinge.

6. Assemble the album by placing the pages in between the front and back covers. Secure with raffia threaded through the punched holes.

7. For the front panel, write the word "photos" with two pencils strapped together, make a stencil, and emboss onto white paper (see page 34 of the *Techniques* book). Add small white labels below your photographs using italic script.

Vasterås 1992

Baby album
sewn in soft fabric

This baby keepsake is made for a girl, but if your new arrival is a boy, simply switch the color palette to blue. The trick is to keep the fabrics neutral.

1. Mark the positions of the two holes in the left-hand side of the paper pages and foam board. Punch the holes.

2. Cover a sheet of foam board with a square of pink silk for the album back cover. Secure in place with double-sided tape (see page 36 in the *Techniques* book).

3. Position a square of felt to line the inside of the back cover and glue in place. Cut out the holes for the binding with a craft knife.

My first steps

My first smile

4. Use the remaining sheet of foam board and score through the reverse side, 1½ in. (6 cm) from the left-hand side to form a hinge. Cover with silk as for the back cover. Add the strip of white linen with the frayed edge toward the center. Line with felt as before.

5. Draw the teddy motif onto cream cotton and stitch around with a zigzag stitch. Work the facial details by hand. Zigzag-stitch a square around the teddy face and trim. Glue in place on the front of the album.

6. Glue an eyelet in place on each binding hole to neaten the edges. Bind the covers and pages together using a length of pink cord threaded through the holes two or three times.

PERSONALIZED JOURNALING
Write information inside the album to record every special moment. Choose upper and lowercase foundation letters in pink gouache.

My first smile

My first steps

Date

Date

R V Z

k y A B C h

D E F G H I

w s J K L M e z

M N O P Q R Q

u n S T U V f v

x W X Y Z

p t a j T i

Alphabet picture

in two different styles

Calligraphy is an art form in its own right. Here, an alphabet is displayed as a vibrant art piece, with a bold blue or yellow theme, to hang in your dining room or enliven a study area.

2. When the paint is dry, rub away the masking fluid with an eraser or your finger.

1. Using an automatic pen and masking fluid, write a flourished alphabet in a vertical design. Once the masking fluid is dry, use a flat brush and quickly sweep cobalt blue gouache over the design. Do not worry about ragged edges.

3. Mix red ochre with a little cobalt blue to make a muted color. Use a No. 3.5 nib and the paint to write smaller letters in upper or lowercase randomly around the design.

1. Draw a right-angled rule with a pencil as a guide on a sheet of white paper. Write the uppercase letters using yellow ochre and a No. 1.5 nib.

2. When dry, use a No. 6 nib and red ochre to write over the alphabet rapidly, adding extended flourishes where appropriate.

3. Finally, as a decorative touch, add a series of red and yellow pen-made diamonds in a variety of sizes.

Resources

Dick Blick Art Materials
P.O. Box 1267
Galesburg, IL 61402-1267
Toll-free: (800) 828-4548
Phone: (309) 343-6181 (Int.)
Website: www.dickblick.com

Jerry's Artarama
5325 Departure Drive
Raleigh, NC 27616
Toll-free: (800) UARTIST (827-8478)
Phone: (919) 878-6782
(in NC)
Website:
www.jerrysartarama.com

Jo-Ann Fabric and Craft Stores, Inc.
2361 Rosecrans Avenue
Suite 360
El Segundo, CA 90245
Toll-free: (800) 525-4951
Website: www.joann.com

Michaels Stores, Inc.
8000 Bent Branch Drive
Irving, TX 75063
Toll-free: (800) MICHAELS
(642-4235)
Website: www.michaels.com

Pearl Paints North America, Inc.
1033 E. Oakland Park Blvd.
Fort Lauderdale, FL 33334
Toll-free: (800) 221-6845
Website: www.pearlart.com

IN CANADA

Curry's Art Store Ltd.
Head Office:
2345 Stanfield Road
Suite 400
Mississauga, ON L4Y 3Y3
Phone: (416) 798-7983
Toll-free: 1-800-268-2969

Loomis Art Store Group
By mail at:
Omer DeSerres
334 St-Catherine Street East
Montreal, Quebec H2X 1L7
Phone: (514) 842-6637
Toll-free: 1-800-363-0318

Mona Lisa Artists' Materials
1518-7th Street SW
Calgary, AB T2R 1A7
Phone: (403) 228-3618
Website:
www.monalisa-artmat.com

IN ASIA

Elephant & Coral Pen Distributors
501 Orchard Road, #02-09A,
Wheelock
Singapore 238880
Phone: 65-7361322
e-mail:
pens@cyberway.com.sg

IN THE UNITED KINGDOM

Hobbycraft, Arts & Crafts Superstore
7 Enterprise Way
Aviation Park
Bournemouth International
Airport, Christchurch
Dorset BH23 6HG
To find a store, call:
0800 0027 2387
Website:
www.hobbycraft.co.uk

Lakeland Ltd.
Alexandria Buildings
Windermere
Cumbria LA23 1BQ
Phone: 01539488100
Website:
www.lakelandlimited.co.uk